I0756349

FINISHING LINE PRESS
www.finishinglinepress.com

The Clarity of Chaos

poems by

Hannah Turner

Finishing Line Press
Georgetown, Kentucky

The Clarity of Chaos

ISBN 979-8-89990-472-1 First Edition

ACKNOWLEDGMENTS

I would like to dedicate this book to my mom. 'Thank you for always jumping into the flames with me.' And also to my family for their ongoing support.

Publisher: Leah Huete de Maines
Editor: Christen Kincaid
Cover Art: Bendan McManus
Author Photo: Alexis Wardius
Cover Design: Elizabeth Maines McCleavy

Order online: www.finishinglinepress.com
also available on amazon.com

Author inquiries and mail orders:
Finishing Line Press
PO Box 1626
Georgetown, Kentucky 40324
USA

Contents

i Darkness

Letter to My First Love

Dear alcohol
You were my very first love
Before any man or woman outside my family
Before I learned how to love myself
There you were

I loved you the way a drowning person loves a floating device
Our first time together created a lightness in me
Mind foggy
Heart protected in a vault
Body free
This is the freedom I once chased as a child

Eyes blurred in the most relaxing of ways
No longer tethered to anything
All pain relinquished
No thoughts or feelings of inferiority
No more shame or sadness for being me

You tied me to my father at a time where there was distance
A dull altered state welcoming us into the flames together
Your burning embrace ventured him and me
down a path of accomplice building
that only grew throughout the years

Your liquid courage led me to tumultuous relations
Dangerous at times

Explicit broken love affairs one after the other
You made me feel special and loved
Grown up when I hadn't done the work to get there

You could also bring death and betrayal
Turning me into a monster who cuts the throats
of anyone who dare take you from me

I was possessed by you
Obsessed
With bloodshot eyes

Racing heart and pounding in my chest
I looked in the mirror and didn't recognize myself
with you by my side

And still when you left, I missed you
in a way I've never missed anyone
I still do from time to time
You almost took my life
and still, I think of you when I'm sad
Or happy
Or neutral
But someday you will be a distant memory
A vice I was engaged with long ago

The Rules of Social Drinking

You must partake
Don't be a party pooper
Don't make people uncomfortable by not drinking
If you want to be included,
you must keep up with everyone
But be able to hold your liquor
Don't ever make a scene by getting sick or falling over
Don't make anyone have to care for you
Don't have too much
Don't have too little
Don't address issues with alcohol
You don't want to be a bummer
With these social rules of drinking
How do we expect anyone to not have a problem?

Self-Serving

Self-serving was my state of being
Asking what would suit me before reaching out to anyone else
What do I need?
What do I want?
Unawareness can act as selfish behavior
The thought of others' needs didn't occur to me in this state
Having the consciousness to see when someone is in need
As people did for me
Awareness has given me this ability

Time in a new, clear consciousness
I see that everyone has pain
I was not special for mine
Stepping outside my circular thoughts
Checking in on my loved ones
Only enhances my own healing
I no longer live in that self-serving state

The Desire to Dissolve

Sinking into something deep and soft
Was all I wanted to do
Giving my mind and body up to a stronger force
Before alcohol it was the television
or playing make believe with plastic dolls.
Turning reality off
and changing the channel to a safe storyline.
One I could control

A time came when I felt I wasn't strong enough.
I grew up and real-world pain grew with me
Staying in the present moment hurt too much.
Pain pushed me out of my body
I crossed a threshold

That sunken place was soon made up of booze
Vodka gin and tequila
built the walls floor and ceiling
of my new home.
Warm fuzzies protected the pain of the present moment.

Blurring my vision and sedating my body
Giving up control of myself
and giving into my desire to dissolve

Don't Try

There was strong, gripping thoughts on rotation to keep me drinking
To keep me sedated
They sounded like:

It's comfortable here isn't it
You have drink to keep you warm and airy
Happy and foggy
Forgetful and fearless

You have money to keep the drink plenty
Never running out
Always free flowing

You have men to keep you company
Giving you love and comfort
Warmth and kindness
Attention which you so badly desire

Lust and filth
Protection and paternity
Fantasy and nightmare
You have it all
Just stay here in limbo until your mind decays with toxins

It Is Not Normal

How many times did I wake up
with fuzzy images from the night before?

When did that become normal?
Daily
Expected

Thinking it's normal to wake up half clothed
not remembering why
is a tragedy
Nothing to be normalized
Or expected

How many souls must leave us
before we see this isn't normal.

The Narratives We Create

Collapsed into a merry go round of our own creation
One that deceives and manipulates
a layer of truth lives within this story
But when stories become the identity
I no longer question its authenticity
relevance is never examined
and this narrative becomes a suit of armor
one that soaks into the skin

Deeper and deeper with each thought rotation
Every time it's taken out and run through my mind
The story gets closer to my heart,
and I don't notice its strong pull
To keep me in a never-ending loop
I told myself the world is scary without alcohol
without drinking, the dangers of life will kill me
I don't have the skill set to function
without the warm embrace of the substance
We all have our narratives we tell ourselves
That was mine

My Childhood Room

What things have happened here?

I played with my toys on the bed in here
I watched movies with my friends in here
I had my first beer and hid it under the bed in here

I cried for my first heartbreak in here
I learned how to create outfits in here

I hid bottles of alcohol under my clothes in the closet in here
I had sex with my first boyfriend in here
I had secret parties in here

I felt safe in here
I felt wild in here

There was a time I felt a tightness in my chest
from all the ghosts in this room
As if the once innocent energy
had been disgraced by secretive actions
taken by my double life.

But now they have drifted with my recovery
I feel at home in my childhood room

If There is No Witness, Am I Real?

My lights turn off when I am alone
I am detached from the light switch
But when I am with a separate pair of eyes
Suddenly I become real flesh and blood
My heart beats and my eyes blink and my breath starts
I exist with eyes on me
As if they are spotlights and I am an actor
When they disappear so do I
As though I only exist for them
Begging the question
If there is no witness, am I real?

Nuanced Love

It's not black and white—
layers of gray.
The beauty, the pain, the frustration
The clearer my mind and body get
The greyer my vision becomes
The grand love affair I once thought
was burning with a sunset glow
is now a confusing mind field

Nothing is certain
Nothing is fact
There are no shapes I can make of the mixed bag
of emotions I get from this love

I have tried to internalize, theorize,
and actualize this experience
I have tried to deny and push away my feelings.
But still there they float
On a dead sea of uncertainty

As I try to accept what I cannot change
I will accept all that is gray

Deer in the Headlights

Doe-eyed bushy tailed
trouble and innocence entangled
in her eyes as she asks for help
as she explains her pain and heartbreak
with lust on her tongue

I don't wish to be her anymore
The doe eyes now see wisdom
The heartache of experience has turned her innocence dark
Her tongue tastes the ash of her adolescence
The deer in the headlights is outgrown

Coexistence

There is depression living in me

There is a heaviness,
my heart is a magnet to the floor.
My legs feel wobbly from walking,
I am so tired but can't sleep

There is anxiety living in me

must be sitting or lying down but always awake and alert
aware of every sound once the sun goes down
trapped in the airless space between my four walls.
Annoyance at the world
in a flavor that tastes of loneliness and fear of isolation.
Fear of being away from the ones I love.
Fear of the pages in front of me as the ones behind
start to erase themselves.

This swing from depression to anxiety
amplified in the beginning months of sobriety
Oscillating between obsession and indifference
Feeling broken by the past
and tortured by what could happen in the future

Over time it has balanced out to a softer
smaller movement back and forth
meeting closer in the middle
These extremes have found a way to coexist

23-Year-Old Woman

There was a time I wanted to do it
To end it all
A time when the world felt too heavy
My body felt too heavy
Thankfully I had someone
A beacon
A lighthouse that led me back to safety

In the time I have been clean I haven't wanted it
The thought of it broke my heart
But for some reason I was pondering the concept tonight
Not the action itself but the idea
What does it mean to take your own life?
What did it feel like for me to want that ending for myself?
Is there any part of me still broken enough to wish I were dead?

Right then a woman came to me
Told me her 23-year-old daughter took her own life
Looking in her eyes
The eyes of a grieving mother
I've never been confronted with grief in this way
Seeing the broken heart,
the unimaginable pain coursing through her body
Struck me like lightning
This is what happens to those left behind
I don't want that for my loved ones

ii Moments

The Morning after a Milestone

Screams flooded my chest
with no way out.
Silent tears and toxins drowned my heart.
The taste erased the pride of growth.
Sorrow and self-punishment
filled the air the next morning,

I've experimented
and received my answer:
I can't have the poison in my body any longer.
Tasting sweet at first
but turned my insides black with ash,
the aggressive fear of repeating the past.

Haven been bitten by this beast once
I decide never again
I received my answer
and let the drink go for good

When I Saw Her Clearly

People don't exist like characters on a screen,
pressing them on when you're lonely
and off when you're full

When Taylor was here, we grasped at our friendship
built on the buzzed fantasy world we created with booze
But seeing her now
with sober clarity,
we unveiled ourselves to one another
without the blankets of alcohol to hide under.

She was a sudden stranger
I was trapped with
There was no button to press her away
No light switch to dim her presence

I saw how lonely I was when I summoned her
The price of fearing myself too deeply
to sit in the discomfort of solitude

Taylor taught me out of this fear
Sitting with oneself brings peace
No external vessel can provide

Wine in the Face

It happened so fast I wasn't sure what it was
I could feel the wetness of iron on my hand then on my face
It's water I thought
Then I smelled the dark damp smell
Panic seeped through my jacket
Under my skin

Painful ugly memories
It wasn't images but recollections
of what the smell brought into my life
Dark shadows started to soar above me as I stood

The waiter that accidentally dropped a full glass of red wine
down the side of my face
standing there in shock and amusement
I couldn't make eye contact with him

Ignoring people's shock and concerns
I walked briskly to the bathroom
I didn't make it in time to lock the door
The tears came up fast with no lead-in

An overflow of trauma with nowhere else to go
No other form than tears and silent screams
I tried to reign it into no avail

Once started, couldn't stop

There would be a time that those tears
would be for my white coat
The sadness of a material object being rained
upon by the blood of wine,
ruined by stains
But the garment was an afterthought

I was being suffocated by the scent of the past

My heart raising and breaking at the same time

The caged bars getting closer
Please don't take me back
please don't take me back I begged

No clear memory came but a known feeling
of isolation and illness on my chest as I gasped for air.

I felt embarrassed and angry
But more than anything I feel sorrow for what was
For everything that that smell was
The very thing I vowed to part ways with was splashed in my face
Forcing me to breath it in
No more

Theatre

We stand outside the theater
I order a gin and tonic
it's the only reason I showed up.
She says I'm the best concert partner
and I'm just thinking of the next round.

Ordering a second, I get carded
Flustered, I tell the truth
Rage fills my veins that I didn't get a refill
Suddenly the cocktail waitress gives me the drink anyway
The relief I feel should be alarming
But all I can focus on is the warmth in my belly.

My mom disperses into the theater
We could only get one ticket
and I agree it should go to her
Generosity?
Maybe not
I want to stay close to the drink cart outside

Men come up to me because of my skimpy attire
We make conversation, I laugh and drink
When My mom returns, the men take us to a bar
I don't like them, but I know they will buy me a drink
My mom is witnessing a side of me she hasn't seen

Entering the bar, he hands me the drink and we talk
I dash out for a bathroom break
on my return, the men are gone
my mother told them I was only 20

On the car ride home tears flood
a pipe burst from holding in too many secrets
My mom has had a first glimpse into my double life
She saw something shocking
A foreign character being portrayed by her daughter
The curtain which held the division between plays
was accidentally pushed open enough for her to catch an eye

full of dangerous plot lines and reckless behavior
There was no anger or disappointment in her eyes
Only empathy and sorrow for my obvious pain
It's going to be alright
I am here for you

Toxic Friendship

As I heat up a chicken sausage for breakfast
I am thrown into a memory of her
We were in my house for a 24-hour party of two
Though I can't remember
I assume it started innocent enough as it always did
Before launching into toxic chaos
She brought out the worst in me
And I her
I remember the bottles of booze
turning into little white lines
I remember the drunken photo shoot
The feeling of wicked adrenaline
that comes with an all-night bender
We had zero self-control together
A tornado effect grabbed hold of our energies
and whipped them around until we were dizzy

My attraction to her was a combination of youthful awe
and dark desire for wild adventure
My inner child was pulled in by her long lashes and sparkly nails,
the way she talked and dressed
My shadow-self viewed her as a partner in crime
Lustful, childlike, mischievous, troublemaker,
all wrapped in one beautiful person
I followed her everywhere
She knew she had me
When it came morning after our bender,
we welcomed the sunrise with another bottle of wine
and put chicken sausages in the microwave

I felt like I was hit by a train
while waiting for the food to heat up.
She wanted to keep the party going
but my conscious came back and urged me to stop
After she left
I ate the sausage on the couch,
trying to keep the room from spinning.
As I stand here now, three years later,

the smell of the chicken sausage
can still drum up that feeling
Of a toxic friendship

Obsession

Addictions come in many forms
People being one type
This feeling took over
when a specific person came into my life
A possessiveness formed around the idea of him
I wanted to call it love
A bright light with the ability to heal all my wounds
But it was more demanding and uncontrollable than that
The lights reflecting in my eyes were in fact
sparks of fatal electricity
Weapons
Spiraling thoughts
Constant scenarios that would never happen
anxiety rising with the thought of this person
Never feeling satisfied after seeing him
Always wanting more attention
More affection
More more more
mirroring the feeling I had with alcohol
Can he save me?
Does he love me?
Can his love make up for the loss of love I had for myself?
I need to do more to get his attention
I need to be more
Say more
Look more
More more more

Putting myself in harmful situations
to be around him
Morphing myself into a shape
I thought would get his attention
All the while not being honest and authentic with him
or myself with what I wanted
My boundaries be damned

Never truly seeing him clearly
Everything I thought he was
was all projection

an ideal man conjured in my mind
based in small moments we shared
Only seeing and hearing what I wanted to be there

Today he is a stranger to me
and always was

I was fixated on a fantasy
Now that is all that lives on

The parallels of this obsession
and the one I had with alcohol
came from the same place
A desire to fulfill the loss of connection
I had with myself

Secrecy as a Form of Intimacy

It makes sense now
that the only relationship that lasted
in the hazy days of my addiction
was with a married man.

An affair paired well with the double life I was living.

Equally exciting as drinking at bars while underage.
The feeling of getting away with risky behavior.
Having a secret that was just between us
allowed me to get close to someone.

As we slowly revealed the ugly parts of ourselves,
love and trust grew.

Lie on top of lie build the walls around us
bringing us closer

Years went by.
Alcohol slowed.
Self-respect came into view
as I gained a wider vantage point.
The ground was shifting underneath us.
Excitement turned to shame and self-loathing.
Our secrets grew darker.
Bedrooms became the back of a car.
Trust and comfort became paranoia and resentment

As you placed a sheet over my body
to hide me from potential known witnesses,
I sunk in the shame of our predicament

There is no longer any light here.
Darkness has seeped through every crevice between us.
Giving me the strength to walk away.
Cutting the web of lies bonding us and putting you in the rearview
mirror

For I will no longer except secrecy as a form of intimacy

I'm Sorry

I had you drive me to the grocery store
when I wanted more bottles
You became accustomed
to seeing me shop for booze.
It felt normal
A sort of bonding time.
I couldn't see how messed up it was back then.
You drove me home and watched me finish each one.

You suggested I stop one night.
Protecting me from myself.
My response?
Getting close to your face
and saying the words
Fuck you

I don't recognize that person anymore
I can't even conjure the memory.
She's a stranger.

I know that's no excuse.

I chose booze over you.
You tried to protect me.
I chose old men over you.
You tried to protect me.
Yet I did nothing to protect you
to shield your eyes from my actions
my inappropriate behavior.

The one who could see what I was doing
I was the cruelest to.
The one who tried to stop it
I ridiculed.

You stood up for me when he put something in my drink.
You confronted him in my honor.
I have not done the same for you
Would I?

I'd like to think I would now
But still, I do not know
For there is no one I have known
that has a heart like yours
I am so sorry for not being the big sister you deserve
I am sorry

The Night I Dropped my Puppy

This was the only time I wanted to relapse
After a year being clean
When our 4-month-old puppy
No bigger than my two hands
Leapt from my grasp
And hit the pavement

As we drove her to the ER
all I wanted to do
was leave my body.
Escape into thin air
Not die
But no longer live
Escape
Disappear
To flee from my chest that became solid armor
hardening and contracting its grip
No way out
No way up
No way down

I was desperate for a release

Even when we returned home
Our puppy in one piece
I couldn't shake the hot fiery guilt and self-loathing
of causing pain to such a delicate being

I tried to sleep
to disassociate
to do something to leave my body besides drink
nothing worked
I had no choice but to sit with this pain
But the next morning I woke to see the clouds parted
What was metal was now soft tissue
Lungs and heart returned to normal
Panic slowed
Sadness was still at attendance
but the presence was a slow and soft one

Sitting lightly in my heart
As if to say
Hello, I'm here and that's okay
You are still you
It's okay that I am here because you made it through the panic
Allow me to sit lightly in your heart and you will be okay

The Repetitive Past

I sat down in the past today
Felt my body in a chair
that threw me into old habits
Unhealthy? Unwise?
Perhaps
A waste of time and energy?
Probably
The scenery was the same
The company I had, the same
I was surrounded by ghosts
And strangers together
A void of what was
And what could have been
If I had been different
Made different choices
5 years later I am different
A changed person
sitting in an unchanged chair
with a barely changed man
Asking myself
Is this what I want to be doing
with my precious new life

iii Emergence

I Don't Miss It

I don't miss it
Not now
Not anymore
I don't miss it
I choose to say no with pride
I don't miss it
I wake up smiling with energy
Thankful I remember the night before
I don't miss it
Not now
Not anymore

It Doesn't Fix Everything

I have made my voice
but still, I am gray.
I have picked a path
but still my spirit feels heavy.

Sobriety has not taken away pain or sadness.
Sobriety has not burned the weight I feel inside.

I thought this road would be sunny
day in and day out.
The sun did come out
but there are still days
I feel blue and cloudy.
There is no hangover
yet my mind is foggy.

As challenging as life can be,
I never wish to drink again
Being clean doesn't fix everything
But nothing is worth going back

Can't Turn Back

You know too much
to ever return to the fantasy you once lived, she said
It doesn't exist anymore

I know those days are gone.
Even if I were to pick up the bottle
they will not come back.

I miss the ignorance and mindless numbing.
When I felt my actions were normal.

But those times don't exist anymore
and ordering a drink will not bring them back.
There is no unknowing where this will lead.
It will only bring sadness from what was and what is.

To Mom

You make me a better, stronger, healthier and happier person.
Feelings are so grand that words feel tiny in comparison.
Thank you is merely too small when expressing my gratitude.

For I would not be where I am without you,
you have saved my life countless times

Lying about my struggles and pain.
I am truly sorry for not seeing how it hurt you

But my heart is at ease
to no longer hide from you

You are my safe space
my lighthouse.
I couldn't see the light
with the dark fog disturbing my vision
I now know you are in my corner, on my team
And you always were

Harm Reduction

The caffeine brings me up in the morning

Where it acted as a hangover cure before
It now gives my body the energy to move quickly in the morning sun
But the heat of the substance burns my cheeks and inflames my belly

Yes, harm reduction is crucial
Just as marijuana doesn't hold the same danger as meth
Caffeine is a smaller threat than booze and cocaine
Yet it is still a drug
Mood altering substance
Pleasurable and energy giving
But hot with electricity and anxiety reproducing
my next step will be to eliminate this stimulant
But for now, I rest in harm reduction

My First Sober Concert

Would I even be fun at a concert without alcohol?
Was I only the best concert partner,
because of the drinking?

Sitting there next to her I was nervous at first
Then the music started, and it all melted away
Our love for the performer rang out
The nerves and self-doubt evaporated with each key stroke

Yet my body felt it was missing something
The space underneath my rib cage felt empty
Cold
no heat, no alterations of any kind
No inflammation, no tugging of toxins
No fire from numbness burning in my chest
hollow
Filled with open space
I was singing and dancing as I always did
Without the altered vice
I can still do this while clean
And better yet, remember it tomorrow

The Liquor Bottle

Feels no different to the touch
Spinning it around in my hands
Scanning my body for a live wire
Strong feelings of fear or excitement
Worry or anger

But no such emotions appear
There is a void of electricity in my chest
No gravitational pull to numb
My impulses are at rest

Is this what it feels like to no longer be owned by this substance?
Is this how it feels to be free of obsession?
Free of cravings?

Impairment once looked like freedom
But it's shackles in a sparkling glistening disguise
Real freedom is a breath
One breath between thought and action

That soon allows for enough distance
to truly see the choices laid out in front of me
The space to observe
what I was opting for then
and what is possible now

Gratitude

A religious person I am not
Religion made me squirm and fidget
With emotions I never quite understood

Religion was a curse word in my head
But coming out of the throws of my addiction
has brought me to my knees in gratitude for my life

Some are not as fortunate
Some do not get as many saves as I did
Most don't get to wake up
after partaking in my actions

Thankful
I am thankful for the trees
for the breath I get to breath
for my resilient soul

Some have turned away from the glare of their reflection
thankful for my courage to stare it in the face
I am thankful for my heartbeat and all it has endured
Gratitude is my religion

My Body

This is my body
I see it as my own
Where it used to be a vessel to get attention,
or alcohol
or whatever it desired
in the moment
Now it is tired and wants to rest
Now it is no one else's
No one commands it or manipulates it
No one overpowers it or dominates it
This body is my own

For my Younger Self

Excitement fills her eyes as the world comes into view for the first time
Vibrant colors and shiny people in shiny places
A fresh glowing smile lights her face
No words come out '
She doesn't talk, she only hugs people
Touch is her only language
Innocent, curious, thoughtful language
With the patience to watch snails move across the driveway
The love to be pen pals with an 80-year-old man
Desiring nothing more than to be included
and not ridiculed or patronized

But being spoken for as a way of protecting her
made her feel ashamed of her development
This feeling grew as she aged into the classroom
Vicious words and harmful actions
dimmed the curious innocent light in her eyes
Terminating the school system rescued her from her peers

But the introduction to alcohol pulled her into a new darkness
At first soft, inviting and healing her wounds
by means of numbness and lack of focus
It began eroding all she held dear without her even noticing

Finally, alone in a city, miles away from home
was she able to put the drink down?
See it for the toxin it was
and not the friend she wanted it to be
18 months have passed
she has gained the excited eyes
and the fresh smile once more
Though she still holds a heavy heart
with all she has seen and felt along the way
Desiring nothing more than to share her story
in the hopes of making those with similar stories
feel less alone

Hannah Turner is a 28-year-old poet living in Ojai, California. She began writing *The Clarity of Chaos* while studying in Paris, where she also began her journey of sobriety. Now three and a half years sober, Hannah channels her experiences with addiction and recovery into poetry that is raw, honest, and deeply human.

www.ingramcontent.com/pod-product-compliance
Lightning Source LLC
LaVergne TN
LVHW090538110826
845146LV00003B/1157

* 9 7 9 8 8 9 9 9 0 4 7 2 1 *